SCORE BOOK

BASEBALL

WITH PITCH COUNT

THIS BOOK BELONGS TO

Starting date	Finished date

SCORE BOOK

BASEBALL

WITH PITCH COUNT

TEAM LINE UP

TEAM	OPPOSING TEAM
COACH	COACH

	NO.	STARTERS	POS.		NO.	SUBSTITUTES	POS
1							
2							
3							
4							
5							
6							
7							
8							
9							
10							
11							
12							
13							
14							
15							
16							
17							

NOTES

DATE	TIME	FIELD

BASEBALL / SOFTBALL SCORESHEET

	#	PLAYER	POS	1	2	3	4	5	6	7	8	9	
1													
SUB.													
2													
SUB.													
3													
SUB.													
4													
SUB.													
5													
SUB.													
6													
SUB.													
7													
SUB.													
8													
SUB.													
9													
SUB.													
10													
SUB.													
11													
SUB.													
12													
SUB.													
13													
SUB.													
14													
SUB.													
15													
SUB.													
16													
SUB.													
17													TOTALS
SUB.													
INNING TOTALS		RUNS											
		HITS											
		ERRORS											
		LEFT ON BASE											

BASEBALL / SOFTBALL SCORESHEET

AB	R	H	RBI	BB	SO	PLAYER #

PLAYER # columns numbered 1–100 (four columns)

DATE	START TIME	END TIME

FIELD

| HOME | |
| VISITOR | |

#	PITCHER	W	L	S	IP	BF	H	R	ER	BB	SO
	TOTALS										

PITCHES BY INNING	1	2	3	4	5	6	7	8	9
TOTALS										

NOTES

FINAL SCORE

	HOME		VISITOR
	RUNS		
	HITS		
	ERRORS		
UMPIRES			
SCORER			

NOTES

PITCH COUNT TOTALS

TEAM LINE UP

TEAM		OPPOSING TEAM	
COACH		COACH	

	NO.	STARTERS	POS.
1			
2			
3			
4			
5			
6			
7			
8			
9			
10			
11			
12			
13			
14			
15			
16			
17			

NO.	SUBSTITUTES	POS

NOTES		
DATE	TIME	FIELD

BASEBALL / SOFTBALL SCORESHEET

	#	PLAYER	POS	1	2	3	4	5	6	7	8	9
1												
SUB.												
2												
SUB.												
3												
SUB.												
4												
SUB.												
5												
SUB.												
6												
SUB.												
7												
SUB.												
8												
SUB.												
9												
SUB.												
10												
SUB.												
11												
SUB.												
12												
SUB.												
13												
SUB.												
14												
SUB.												
15												
SUB.												
16												
SUB.												
17												TOTALS
SUB.												

INNING TOTALS		RUNS										
		HITS										
		ERRORS										
		LEFT ON BASE										

BASEBALL / SOFTBALL SCORESHEET

AB	R	H	RBI	BB	SO	PLAYER #

PLAYER # columns: 1–100 (four columns each numbered 1 through 100)

NOTES

PITCH COUNT TOTALS

DATE	START TIME	END TIME
FIELD		

HOME	
VISITOR	

#	PITCHER	W	L	S	IP	BF	H	R	ER	BB	SO
	TOTALS										

PITCHES BY INNING	1	2	3	4	5	6	7	8	9
TOTALS									

NOTES

FINAL SCORE

	HOME	VISITOR
	RUNS	
	HITS	
	ERRORS	

UMPIRES	
SCORER	

TEAM LINE UP

TEAM		OPPOSING TEAM	
COACH		COACH	

	NO.	STARTERS	POS.		NO.	SUBSTITUTES	POS
1							
2							
3							
4							
5							
6							
7							
8							
9							
10							
11							
12							
13							
14							
15							
16							
17							

NOTES		
DATE	TIME	FIELD

BASEBALL / SOFTBALL SCORESHEET

	#	PLAYER	POS	1	2	3	4	5	6	7	8	9
1												
SUB.												
2												
SUB.												
3												
SUB.												
4												
SUB.												
5												
SUB.												
6												
SUB.												
7												
SUB.												
8												
SUB.												
9												
SUB.												
10												
SUB.												
11												
SUB.												
12												
SUB.												
13												
SUB.												
14												
SUB.												
15												
SUB.												
16												
SUB.												
17												
SUB.												TOTALS

INNING TOTALS	RUNS									
	HITS									
	ERRORS									
	LEFT ON BASE									

Each inning cell header: 1B 2B 3B HR BB

BASEBALL / SOFTBALL SCORESHEET

AB	R	H	RBI	BB	SO		PLAYER #		
						1 / 1 / 1 / 1			
						2–100			

DATE		START TIME		END TIME	
FIELD					
HOME					
VISITOR					

#	PITCHER	W	L	S	IP	BF	H	R	ER	BB	SO
	TOTALS										

PITCHES BY INNING	1	2	3	4	5	6	7	8	9
TOTALS									

NOTES

FINAL SCORE	
HOME	VISITOR
RUNS	
HITS	
ERRORS	
UMPIRES	
SCORER	

NOTES

PITCH COUNT TOTALS

TEAM LINE UP

TEAM	OPPOSING TEAM
COACH	COACH

	NO.	STARTERS	POS.		NO.	SUBSTITUTES	POS
1							
2							
3							
4							
5							
6							
7							
8							
9							
10							
11							
12							
13							
14							
15							
16							
17							

NOTES

DATE	TIME	FIELD

BASEBALL / SOFTBALL SCORESHEET

	#	PLAYER	POS	1	2	3	4	5	6	7	8	9
1												
SUB.												
2												
SUB.												
3												
SUB.												
4												
SUB.												
5												
SUB.												
6												
SUB.												
7												
SUB.												
8												
SUB.												
9												
SUB.												
10												
SUB.												
11												
SUB.												
12												
SUB.												
13												
SUB.												
14												
SUB.												
15												
SUB.												
16												
SUB.												
17													TOTALS
SUB.												

INNING TOTALS	RUNS									
	HITS									
	ERRORS									
	LEFT ON BASE									

BASEBALL / SOFTBALL SCORESHEET

AB	R	H	RBI	BB	SO	PLAYER #

PLAYER # columns:

1	1	1	1
2	2	2	2
3	3	3	3
4	4	4	4
5	5	5	5
6	6	6	6
7	7	7	7
8	8	8	8
9	9	9	9
10	10	10	10
11	11	11	11
12	12	12	12
13	13	13	13
14	14	14	14
15	15	15	15
16	16	16	16
17	17	17	17
18	18	18	18
19	19	19	19
20	20	20	20
21	21	21	21
22	22	22	22
23	23	23	23
24	24	24	24
25	25	25	25
26	26	26	26
27	27	27	27
28	28	28	28
29	29	29	29
30	30	30	30
31	31	31	31
32	32	32	32
33	33	33	33
34	34	34	34
35	35	35	35
36	36	36	36
37	37	37	37
38	38	38	38
39	39	39	39
40	40	40	40
41	41	41	41
42	42	42	42
43	43	43	43
44	44	44	44
45	45	45	45
46	46	46	46
47	47	47	47
48	48	48	48
49	49	49	49
50	50	50	50
51	51	51	51
52	52	52	52
53	53	53	53
54	54	54	54
55	55	55	55
56	56	56	56
57	57	57	57
58	58	58	58
59	59	59	59
60	60	60	60
61	61	61	61
62	62	62	62
63	63	63	63
64	64	64	64
65	65	65	65
66	66	66	66
67	67	67	67
68	68	68	68
69	69	69	69
70	70	70	70
71	71	71	71
72	72	72	72
73	73	73	73
74	74	74	74
75	75	75	75
76	76	76	76
77	77	77	77
78	78	78	78
79	79	79	79
80	80	80	80
81	81	81	81
82	82	82	82
83	83	83	83
84	84	84	84
85	85	85	85
86	86	86	86
87	87	87	87
88	88	88	88
89	89	89	89
90	90	90	90
91	91	91	91
92	92	92	92
93	93	93	93
94	94	94	94
95	95	95	95
96	96	96	96
97	97	97	97
98	98	98	98
99	99	99	99
100	100	100	100

NOTES

PITCH COUNT TOTALS

DATE

START TIME

END TIME

FIELD

HOME

VISITOR

#	PITCHER	W	L	S	IP	BF	H	R	ER	BB	SO
	TOTALS										

PITCHES BY INNING	1	2	3	4	5	6	7	8	9
TOTALS									

NOTES

FINAL SCORE

HOME		VISITOR
	RUNS	
	HITS	
	ERRORS	

UMPIRES

SCORER

TEAM LINE UP

TEAM	OPPOSING TEAM
COACH	COACH

	NO.	STARTERS	POS.
1			
2			
3			
4			
5			
6			
7			
8			
9			
10			
11			
12			
13			
14			
15			
16			
17			

NO.	SUBSTITUTES	POS

NOTES		
DATE	TIME	FIELD

BASEBALL / SOFTBALL SCORESHEET

	#	PLAYER	POS	1	2	3	4	5	6	7	8	9
1												
SUB.												
2												
SUB.												
3												
SUB.												
4												
SUB.												
5												
SUB.												
6												
SUB.												
7												
SUB.												
8												
SUB.												
9												
SUB.												
10												
SUB.												
11												
SUB.												
12												
SUB.												
13												
SUB.												
14												
SUB.												
15												
SUB.												
16												
SUB.												
17												
SUB.												TOTALS

Each inning cell contains: 1B 2B 3B HR BB

INNING TOTALS	RUNS									
	HITS									
	ERRORS									
	LEFT ON BASE									

BASEBALL / SOFTBALL SCORESHEET

AB	R	H	RBI	BB	SO	PLAYER #			
						1 2 3 ... 100	1 2 3 ... 100	1 2 3 ... 100	1 2 3 ... 100

NOTES

PITCH COUNT TOTALS

DATE	START TIME	END TIME
FIELD		

HOME	
VISITOR	

#	PITCHER	W	L	S	IP	BF	H	R	ER	BB	SO
	TOTALS										

PITCHES BY INNING	1	2	3	4	5	6	7	8	9
TOTALS									

NOTES

FINAL SCORE	
HOME	VISITOR
RUNS	
HITS	
ERRORS	
UMPIRES	
SCORER	

TEAM LINE UP

TEAM		OPPOSING TEAM	
COACH		COACH	

	NO.	STARTERS	POS.
1			
2			
3			
4			
5			
6			
7			
8			
9			
10			
11			
12			
13			
14			
15			
16			
17			

NO.	SUBSTITUTES	POS

NOTES		
DATE	TIME	FIELD

BASEBALL / SOFTBALL SCORESHEET

	#	PLAYER	POS	1	2	3	4	5	6	7	8	9	
1													
SUB.													
2													
SUB.													
3													
SUB.													
4													
SUB.													
5													
SUB.													
6													
SUB.													
7													
SUB.													
8													
SUB.													
9													
SUB.													
10													
SUB.													
11													
SUB.													
12													
SUB.													
13													
SUB.													
14													
SUB.													
15													
SUB.													
16													
SUB.													
17													TOTALS
SUB.													
INNING TOTALS		RUNS											
		HITS											
		ERRORS											
		LEFT ON BASE											

BASEBALL / SOFTBALL SCORESHEET

AB	R	H	RBI	BB	SO		PLAYER #			

PLAYER #

1	1	1	1
2	2	2	2
3	3	3	3
4	4	4	4
5	5	5	5
6	6	6	6
7	7	7	7
8	8	8	8
9	9	9	9
10	10	10	10
11	11	11	11
12	12	12	12
13	13	13	13
14	14	14	14
15	15	15	15
16	16	16	16
17	17	17	17
18	18	18	18
19	19	19	19
20	20	20	20
21	21	21	21
22	22	22	22
23	23	23	23
24	24	24	24
25	25	25	25
26	26	26	26
27	27	27	27
28	28	28	28
29	29	29	29
30	30	30	30
31	31	31	31
32	32	32	32
33	33	33	33
34	34	34	34
35	35	35	35
36	36	36	36
37	37	37	37
38	38	38	38
39	39	39	39
40	40	40	40
41	41	41	41
42	42	42	42
43	43	43	43
44	44	44	44
45	45	45	45
46	46	46	46
47	47	47	47
48	48	48	48
49	49	49	49
50	50	50	50
51	51	51	51
52	52	52	52
53	53	53	53
54	54	54	54
55	55	55	55
56	56	56	56
57	57	57	57
58	58	58	58
59	59	59	59
60	60	60	60
61	61	61	61
62	62	62	62
63	63	63	63
64	64	64	64
65	65	65	65
66	66	66	66
67	67	67	67
68	68	68	68
69	69	69	69
70	70	70	70
71	71	71	71
72	72	72	72
73	73	73	73
74	74	74	74
75	75	75	75
76	76	76	76
77	77	77	77
78	78	78	78
79	79	79	79
80	80	80	80
81	81	81	81
82	82	82	82
83	83	83	83
84	84	84	84
85	85	85	85
86	86	86	86
87	87	87	87
88	88	88	88
89	89	89	89
90	90	90	90
91	91	91	91
92	92	92	92
93	93	93	93
94	94	94	94
95	95	95	95
96	96	96	96
97	97	97	97
98	98	98	98
99	99	99	99
100	100	100	100

NOTES

PITCH COUNT TOTALS

DATE	START TIME	END TIME

FIELD

HOME	
VISITOR	

#	PITCHER	W	L	S	IP	BF	H	R	ER	BB	SO
	TOTALS										

PITCHES BY INNING	1	2	3	4	5	6	7	8	9
TOTALS									

NOTES

FINAL SCORE		
HOME		VISITOR
	RUNS	
	HITS	
	ERRORS	
UMPIRES		
SCORER		

TEAM LINE UP

TEAM	OPPOSING TEAM
COACH	COACH

	NO.	STARTERS	POS.		NO.	SUBSTITUTES	POS
1							
2							
3							
4							
5							
6							
7							
8							
9							
10							
11							
12							
13							
14							
15							
16							
17							

NOTES

DATE	TIME	FIELD

BASEBALL / SOFTBALL SCORESHEET

	#	PLAYER	POS	1	2	3	4	5	6	7	8	9
1												
SUB.												
2												
SUB.												
3												
SUB.												
4												
SUB.												
5												
SUB.												
6												
SUB.												
7												
SUB.												
8												
SUB.												
9												
SUB.												
10												
SUB.												
11												
SUB.												
12												
SUB.												
13												
SUB.												
14												
SUB.												
15												
SUB.												
16												
SUB.												
17												
SUB.												TOTALS

INNING TOTALS	RUNS									
	HITS									
	ERRORS									
	LEFT ON BASE									

BASEBALL / SOFTBALL SCORESHEET

AB	R	H	RBI	BB	SO	PLAYER #			
						1 1 1 1			
						2 2 2 2			
						3 3 3 3			
						4 4 4 4			
						5 5 5 5			
						6 6 6 6			
						7 7 7 7			
						8 8 8 8			
						9 9 9 9			
						10 10 10 10			

(Player number columns continue numbered 1 through 100 down the page.)

NOTES

PITCH COUNT TOTALS

DATE	START TIME	END TIME
FIELD		

HOME	
VISITOR	

#	PITCHER	W	L	S	IP	BF	H	R	ER	BB	SO
	TOTALS										

PITCHES BY INNING	1	2	3	4	5	6	7	8	9
TOTALS									

NOTES

FINAL SCORE	
HOME	VISITOR
	RUNS	
	HITS	
	ERRORS	
UMPIRES	
SCORER	

TEAM LINE UP

TEAM	OPPOSING TEAM
COACH	COACH

	NO.	STARTERS	POS.		NO.	SUBSTITUTES	POS
1							
2							
3							
4							
5							
6							
7							
8							
9							
10							
11							
12							
13							
14							
15							
16							
17							

NOTES

DATE	TIME	FIELD

BASEBALL / SOFTBALL SCORESHEET

	#	PLAYER	POS	1	2	3	4	5	6	7	8	9
1												
SUB.												
2												
SUB.												
3												
SUB.												
4												
SUB.												
5												
SUB.												
6												
SUB.												
7												
SUB.												
8												
SUB.												
9												
SUB.												
10												
SUB.												
11												
SUB.												
12												
SUB.												
13												
SUB.												
14												
SUB.												
15												
SUB.												
16												
SUB.												
17												
SUB.												

INNING TOTALS										
	RUNS									
	HITS									
	ERRORS									
	LEFT ON BASE									

TOTALS

BASEBALL / SOFTBALL SCORESHEET

AB	R	H	RBI	BB	SO	PLAYER #

PLAYER # columns: four columns each numbered 1 through 100

DATE	START TIME	END TIME

FIELD

HOME	
VISITOR	

#	PITCHER	W	L	S	IP	BF	H	R	ER	BB	SO
	TOTALS										

PITCHES BY INNING	1	2	3	4	5	6	7	8	9
TOTALS									

NOTES

FINAL SCORE

	HOME		VISITOR
	RUNS		
	HITS		
	ERRORS		

UMPIRES	
SCORER	

NOTES

PITCH COUNT TOTALS

TEAM LINE UP

TEAM	OPPOSING TEAM
COACH	COACH

	NO.	STARTERS	POS.		NO.	SUBSTITUTES	POS
1							
2							
3							
4							
5							
6							
7							
8							
9							
10							
11							
12							
13							
14							
15							
16							
17							

NOTES

DATE	TIME	FIELD

BASEBALL / SOFTBALL SCORESHEET

	#	PLAYER	POS	1	2	3	4	5	6	7	8	9
1												
SUB.												
2												
SUB.												
3												
SUB.												
4												
SUB.												
5												
SUB.												
6												
SUB.												
7												
SUB.												
8												
SUB.												
9												
SUB.												
10												
SUB.												
11												
SUB.												
12												
SUB.												
13												
SUB.												
14												
SUB.												
15												
SUB.												
16												
SUB.												
17												
SUB.												TOTALS

INNING TOTALS		RUNS										
		HITS										
		ERRORS										
		LEFT ON BASE										

BASEBALL / SOFTBALL SCORESHEET

AB	R	H	RBI	BB	SO	PLAYER #

Player count columns numbered 1–100 (four columns).

NOTES

PITCH COUNT TOTALS

DATE	START TIME	END TIME

FIELD

HOME	
VISITOR	

#	PITCHER	W	L	S	IP	BF	H	R	ER	BB	SO
	TOTALS										

PITCHES BY INNING	1	2	3	4	5	6	7	8	9
TOTALS									

NOTES

FINAL SCORE	
HOME	VISITOR
RUNS	
HITS	
ERRORS	
UMPIRES	
SCORER	

TEAM LINE UP

TEAM		OPPOSING TEAM	
COACH		COACH	

	NO.	STARTERS	POS.
1			
2			
3			
4			
5			
6			
7			
8			
9			
10			
11			
12			
13			
14			
15			
16			
17			

NO.	SUBSTITUTES	POS

NOTES		
DATE	TIME	FIELD

BASEBALL / SOFTBALL SCORESHEET

	#	PLAYER	POS	1	2	3	4	5	6	7	8	9
1												
SUB.												
2												
SUB.												
3												
SUB.												
4												
SUB.												
5												
SUB.												
6												
SUB.												
7												
SUB.												
8												
SUB.												
9												
SUB.												
10												
SUB.												
11												
SUB.												
12												
SUB.												
13												
SUB.												
14												
SUB.												
15												
SUB.												
16												
SUB.												
17												TOTALS
SUB.												

INNING TOTALS	RUNS									
	HITS									
	ERRORS									
	LEFT ON BASE									

BASEBALL / SOFTBALL SCORESHEET

AB	R	H	RBI	BB	SO	PLAYER #

PLAYER # columns: 1-100 (four columns, each numbered 1 through 100)

NOTES

PITCH COUNT TOTALS

DATE	START TIME	END TIME

FIELD

HOME	
VISITOR	

#	PITCHER	W	L	S	IP	BF	H	R	ER	BB	SO
	TOTALS										

PITCHES BY INNING	1	2	3	4	5	6	7	8	9
TOTALS									

NOTES

FINAL SCORE	
HOME	VISITOR
RUNS	
HITS	
ERRORS	

UMPIRES	
SCORER	

TEAM LINE UP

TEAM		OPPOSING TEAM	
COACH		COACH	

	NO.	STARTERS	POS.		NO.	SUBSTITUTES	POS
1							
2							
3							
4							
5							
6							
7							
8							
9							
10							
11							
12							
13							
14							
15							
16							
17							

NOTES

DATE	TIME	FIELD

BASEBALL / SOFTBALL SCORESHEET

	#	PLAYER	POS	1	2	3	4	5	6	7	8	9
1												
SUB.												
2												
SUB.												
3												
SUB.												
4												
SUB.												
5												
SUB.												
6												
SUB.												
7												
SUB.												
8												
SUB.												
9												
SUB.												
10												
SUB.												
11												
SUB.												
12												
SUB.												
13												
SUB.												
14												
SUB.												
15												
SUB.												
16												
SUB.												
17												
SUB.												TOTALS

INNING TOTALS	RUNS									
	HITS									
	ERRORS									
	LEFT ON BASE									

Each batter cell is marked with: 1B 2B 3B HR BB

BASEBALL / SOFTBALL SCORESHEET

AB	R	H	RBI	BB	SO		PLAYER #			

PLAYER # columns numbered 1–100 (four columns, each 1 through 100)

NOTES

PITCH COUNT TOTALS

DATE	START TIME	END TIME

FIELD

HOME	
VISITOR	

#	PITCHER	W	L	S	IP	BF	H	R	ER	BB	SO
	TOTALS										

PITCHES BY INNING	1	2	3	4	5	6	7	8	9
TOTALS									

NOTES

FINAL SCORE	
HOME	VISITOR
RUNS	
HITS	
ERRORS	

UMPIRES	
SCORER	

TEAM LINE UP

TEAM	OPPOSING TEAM
COACH	COACH

	NO.	STARTERS	POS.
1			
2			
3			
4			
5			
6			
7			
8			
9			
10			
11			
12			
13			
14			
15			
16			
17			

	NO.	SUBSTITUTES	POS

NOTES

DATE	TIME	FIELD

BASEBALL / SOFTBALL SCORESHEET

	#	PLAYER	POS	1	2	3	4	5	6	7	8	9
1												
SUB.												
2												
SUB.												
3												
SUB.												
4												
SUB.												
5												
SUB.												
6												
SUB.												
7												
SUB.												
8												
SUB.												
9												
SUB.												
10												
SUB.												
11												
SUB.												
12												
SUB.												
13												
SUB.												
14												
SUB.												
15												
SUB.												
16												
SUB.												
17												
SUB.												TOTALS

INNING TOTALS	RUNS										
	HITS										
	ERRORS										
	LEFT ON BASE										

BASEBALL / SOFTBALL SCORESHEET

AB	R	H	RBI	BB	SO	PLAYER #				

(Player tally columns numbered 1–100 in four columns)

NOTES

PITCH COUNT TOTALS

DATE	START TIME	END TIME
FIELD		

HOME	
VISITOR	

#	PITCHER	W	L	S	IP	BF	H	R	ER	BB	SO
	TOTALS										

PITCHES BY INNING	1	2	3	4	5	6	7	8	9
TOTALS									

NOTES

FINAL SCORE		
HOME		VISITOR
	RUNS	
	HITS	
	ERRORS	
UMPIRES		
SCORER		

TEAM LINE UP

TEAM		OPPOSING TEAM	
COACH		COACH	

	NO.	STARTERS	POS.
1			
2			
3			
4			
5			
6			
7			
8			
9			
10			
11			
12			
13			
14			
15			
16			
17			

NO.	SUBSTITUTES	POS

NOTES

DATE	TIME	FIELD

BASEBALL / SOFTBALL SCORESHEET

	#	PLAYER	POS	1	2	3	4	5	6	7	8	9
1												
SUB.												
2												
SUB.												
3												
SUB.												
4												
SUB.												
5												
SUB.												
6												
SUB.												
7												
SUB.												
8												
SUB.												
9												
SUB.												
10												
SUB.												
11												
SUB.												
12												
SUB.												
13												
SUB.												
14												
SUB.												
15												
SUB.												
16												
SUB.												
17												
SUB.												TOTALS

INNING TOTALS	RUNS											
	HITS											
	ERRORS											
	LEFT ON BASE											

Each inning cell header reads: 1B 2B 3B HR BB

BASEBALL / SOFTBALL SCORESHEET

AB	R	H	RBI	BB	SO

PLAYER #

1 2 3 4 5 6 7 8 9 10 11 12 13 14 15 16 17 18 19 20 21 22 23 24 25 26 27 28 29 30 31 32 33 34 35 36 37 38 39 40 41 42 43 44 45 46 47 48 49 50 51 52 53 54 55 56 57 58 59 60 61 62 63 64 65 66 67 68 69 70 71 72 73 74 75 76 77 78 79 80 81 82 83 84 85 86 87 88 89 90 91 92 93 94 95 96 97 98 99 100

NOTES

PITCH COUNT TOTALS

DATE	START TIME	END TIME

FIELD

HOME	
VISITOR	

#	PITCHER	W	L	S	IP	BF	H	R	ER	BB	SO
	TOTALS										

PITCHES BY INNING	1	2	3	4	5	6	7	8	9
TOTALS									

NOTES

FINAL SCORE

HOME	VISITOR
	RUNS	
	HITS	
	ERRORS	

UMPIRES	
SCORER	

TEAM LINE UP

TEAM		OPPOSING TEAM	
COACH		COACH	

	NO.	STARTERS	POS.		NO.	SUBSTITUTES	POS
1							
2							
3							
4							
5							
6							
7							
8							
9							
10							
11							
12							
13							
14							
15							
16							
17							

NOTES		
DATE	TIME	FIELD

BASEBALL / SOFTBALL SCORESHEET

	#	PLAYER	POS	1	2	3	4	5	6	7	8	9
1												
SUB.												
2												
SUB.												
3												
SUB.												
4												
SUB.												
5												
SUB.												
6												
SUB.												
7												
SUB.												
8												
SUB.												
9												
SUB.												
10												
SUB.												
11												
SUB.												
12												
SUB.												
13												
SUB.												
14												
SUB.												
15												
SUB.												
16												
SUB.												
17												
SUB.												TOTALS

INNING TOTALS	RUNS									
	HITS									
	ERRORS									
	LEFT ON BASE									

BASEBALL / SOFTBALL SCORESHEET

AB	R	H	RBI	BB	SO	PLAYER #

PLAYER # columns: 1–100 (four columns each numbered 1 through 100)

NOTES

PITCH COUNT TOTALS

DATE	START TIME	END TIME

FIELD

HOME	
VISITOR	

#	PITCHER	W	L	S	IP	BF	H	R	ER	BB	SO
	TOTALS										

PITCHES BY INNING	1	2	3	4	5	6	7	8	9
TOTALS										

NOTES

FINAL SCORE	
HOME	VISITOR

	RUNS	
	HITS	
	ERRORS	

UMPIRES	
SCORER	

TEAM LINE UP

TEAM	OPPOSING TEAM
COACH	COACH

	NO.	STARTERS	POS.		NO.	SUBSTITUTES	POS
1							
2							
3							
4							
5							
6							
7							
8							
9							
10							
11							
12							
13							
14							
15							
16							
17							

NOTES

DATE	TIME	FIELD

BASEBALL / SOFTBALL SCORESHEET

	#	PLAYER	POS	1	2	3	4	5	6	7	8	9	
1													
SUB.													
2													
SUB.													
3													
SUB.													
4													
SUB.													
5													
SUB.													
6													
SUB.													
7													
SUB.													
8													
SUB.													
9													
SUB.													
10													
SUB.													
11													
SUB.													
12													
SUB.													
13													
SUB.													
14													
SUB.													
15													
SUB.													
16													
SUB.													
17														TOTALS
SUB.													

INNING TOTALS	RUNS									
	HITS									
	ERRORS									
	LEFT ON BASE									

BASEBALL / SOFTBALL SCORESHEET

						PLAYER #			
AB	R	H	RBI	BB	SO				
						1	1	1	1
						2	2	2	2
						3	3	3	3
						4	4	4	4
						5	5	5	5
						6	6	6	6
						7	7	7	7
						8	8	8	8
						9	9	9	9
						10	10	10	10
						11	11	11	11
						12	12	12	12
						13	13	13	13
						14	14	14	14
						15	15	15	15
						16	16	16	16
						17	17	17	17
						18	18	18	18
						19	19	19	19
						20	20	20	20
						21	21	21	21
						22	22	22	22
						23	23	23	23
						24	24	24	24
						25	25	25	25
						26	26	26	26
						27	27	27	27
						28	28	28	28
						29	29	29	29
						30	30	30	30
						31	31	31	31
						32	32	32	32
						33	33	33	33
						34	34	34	34
						35	35	35	35
						36	36	36	36
						37	37	37	37
						38	38	38	38
						39	39	39	39
						40	40	40	40
						41	41	41	41
						42	42	42	42
						43	43	43	43
						44	44	44	44
						45	45	45	45
						46	46	46	46
						47	47	47	47
						48	48	48	48
						49	49	49	49
						50	50	50	50
						51	51	51	51
						52	52	52	52
						53	53	53	53
						54	54	54	54
						55	55	55	55
						56	56	56	56
						57	57	57	57
						58	58	58	58
						59	59	59	59
						60	60	60	60
						61	61	61	61
						62	62	62	62
						63	63	63	63
						64	64	64	64
						65	65	65	65
						66	66	66	66
						67	67	67	67
						68	68	68	68
						69	69	69	69
						70	70	70	70
						71	71	71	71
						72	72	72	72
						73	73	73	73
						74	74	74	74
						75	75	75	75
						76	76	76	76
						77	77	77	77
						78	78	78	78
						79	79	79	79
						80	80	80	80
						81	81	81	81
						82	82	82	82
						83	83	83	83
						84	84	84	84
						85	85	85	85
						86	86	86	86
						87	87	87	87
						88	88	88	88
						89	89	89	89
						90	90	90	90
						91	91	91	91
						92	92	92	92
						93	93	93	93
						94	94	94	94
						95	95	95	95
						96	96	96	96
						97	97	97	97
						98	98	98	98
						99	99	99	99
						100	100	100	100
NOTES						PITCH COUNT TOTALS			

DATE	START TIME	END TIME
FIELD		
HOME		
VISITOR		

#	PITCHER	W	L	S	IP	BF	H	R	ER	BB	SO
TOTALS											

PITCHES BY INNING	1	2	3	4	5	6	7	8	9
TOTALS									

NOTES

FINAL SCORE		
HOME		VISITOR
	RUNS	
	HITS	
	ERRORS	
UMPIRES		
SCORER		

TEAM LINE UP

TEAM	OPPOSING TEAM
COACH	COACH

	NO.	STARTERS	POS.		NO.	SUBSTITUTES	POS
1							
2							
3							
4							
5							
6							
7							
8							
9							
10							
11							
12							
13							
14							
15							
16							
17							

NOTES		
DATE	TIME	FIELD

BASEBALL / SOFTBALL SCORESHEET

	#	PLAYER	POS	1	2	3	4	5	6	7	8	9
1												
SUB.												
2												
SUB.												
3												
SUB.												
4												
SUB.												
5												
SUB.												
6												
SUB.												
7												
SUB.												
8												
SUB.												
9												
SUB.												
10												
SUB.												
11												
SUB.												
12												
SUB.												
13												
SUB.												
14												
SUB.												
15												
SUB.												
16												
SUB.												
17												
SUB.												

TOTALS

INNING TOTALS			
	RUNS		
	HITS		
	ERRORS		
	LEFT ON BASE		

BASEBALL / SOFTBALL SCORESHEET

AB	R	H	RBI	BB	SO	PLAYER #

PLAYER # columns (1–100 repeated in four columns)

DATE	START TIME	END TIME

FIELD

HOME	
VISITOR	

#	PITCHER	W	L	S	IP	BF	H	R	ER	BB	SO
	TOTALS										

PITCHES BY INNING	1	2	3	4	5	6	7	8	9
TOTALS									

NOTES

FINAL SCORE		
HOME		VISITOR
	RUNS	
	HITS	
	ERRORS	
UMPIRES		
SCORER		

NOTES

PITCH COUNT TOTALS

TEAM LINE UP

TEAM	OPPOSING TEAM
COACH	COACH

	NO.	STARTERS	POS.		NO.	SUBSTITUTES	POS
1							
2							
3							
4							
5							
6							
7							
8							
9							
10							
11							
12							
13							
14							
15							
16							
17							

NOTES		
DATE	TIME	FIELD

BASEBALL / SOFTBALL SCORESHEET

	#	PLAYER	POS	1	2	3	4	5	6	7	8	9
1												
SUB.												
2												
SUB.												
3												
SUB.												
4												
SUB.												
5												
SUB.												
6												
SUB.												
7												
SUB.												
8												
SUB.												
9												
SUB.												
10												
SUB.												
11												
SUB.												
12												
SUB.												
13												
SUB.												
14												
SUB.												
15												
SUB.												
16												
SUB.												
17												
SUB.												TOTALS

INNING TOTALS		RUNS											
		HITS											
		ERRORS											
		LEFT ON BASE											

BASEBALL / SOFTBALL SCORESHEET

AB	R	H	RBI	BB	SO	PLAYER #

PLAYER # columns:

1	1	1	1
2	2	2	2
3	3	3	3
4	4	4	4
5	5	5	5
6	6	6	6
7	7	7	7
8	8	8	8
9	9	9	9
10	10	10	10
11	11	11	11
12	12	12	12
13	13	13	13
14	14	14	14
15	15	15	15
16	16	16	16
17	17	17	17
18	18	18	18
19	19	19	19
20	20	20	20
21	21	21	21
22	22	22	22
23	23	23	23
24	24	24	24
25	25	25	25
26	26	26	26
27	27	27	27
28	28	28	28
29	29	29	29
30	30	30	30
31	31	31	31
32	32	32	32
33	33	33	33
34	34	34	34
35	35	35	35
36	36	36	36
37	37	37	37
38	38	38	38
39	39	39	39
40	40	40	40
41	41	41	41
42	42	42	42
43	43	43	43
44	44	44	44
45	45	45	45
46	46	46	46
47	47	47	47
48	48	48	48
49	49	49	49
50	50	50	50
51	51	51	51
52	52	52	52
53	53	53	53
54	54	54	54
55	55	55	55
56	56	56	56
57	57	57	57
58	58	58	58
59	59	59	59
60	60	60	60
61	61	61	61
62	62	62	62
63	63	63	63
64	64	64	64
65	65	65	65
66	66	66	66
67	67	67	67
68	68	68	68
69	69	69	69
70	70	70	70
71	71	71	71
72	72	72	72
73	73	73	73
74	74	74	74
75	75	75	75
76	76	76	76
77	77	77	77
78	78	78	78
79	79	79	79
80	80	80	80
81	81	81	81
82	82	82	82
83	83	83	83
84	84	84	84
85	85	85	85
86	86	86	86
87	87	87	87
88	88	88	88
89	89	89	89
90	90	90	90
91	91	91	91
92	92	92	92
93	93	93	93
94	94	94	94
95	95	95	95
96	96	96	96
97	97	97	97
98	98	98	98
99	99	99	99
100	100	100	100

NOTES

PITCH COUNT TOTALS

DATE	START TIME	END TIME

HELD

HOME	
VISITOR	

#	PITCHER	W	L	S	IP	BF	H	R	ER	BB	SO
	TOTALS										

PITCHES BY INNING	1	2	3	4	5	6	7	8	9
TOTALS									

NOTES

FINAL SCORE

HOME		VISITOR
	RUNS	
	HITS	
	ERRORS	
UMPIRES		
SCORER		

TEAM LINE UP

TEAM		OPPOSING TEAM	
COACH		COACH	

	NO.	STARTERS	POS.		NO.	SUBSTITUTES	POS
1							
2							
3							
4							
5							
6							
7							
8							
9							
10							
11							
12							
13							
14							
15							
16							
17							

NOTES		
DATE	TIME	FIELD

BASEBALL / SOFTBALL SCORESHEET

#	PLAYER	POS	1	2	3	4	5	6	7	8	9
1											
SUB.											
2											
SUB.											
3											
SUB.											
4											
SUB.											
5											
SUB.											
6											
SUB.											
7											
SUB.											
8											
SUB.											
9											
SUB.											
10											
SUB.											
11											
SUB.											
12											
SUB.											
13											
SUB.											
14											
SUB.											
15											
SUB.											
16											
SUB.											
17											
SUB.											TOTALS

INNING TOTALS	RUNS										
	HITS										
	ERRORS										
	LEFT ON BASE										

BASEBALL / SOFTBALL SCORESHEET

AB	R	H	RBI	BB	SO	PLAYER #			

PLAYER # columns numbered 1–100 (four columns)

DATE	START TIME	END TIME
FIELD		

HOME	
VISITOR	

#	PITCHER	W	L	S	IP	BF	H	R	ER	BB	SO
	TOTALS										

PITCHES BY INNING	1	2	3	4	5	6	7	8	9
TOTALS									

NOTES

FINAL SCORE

	HOME		VISITOR
	RUNS		
	HITS		
	ERRORS		
UMPIRES			
SCORER			

NOTES

PITCH COUNT TOTALS

TEAM LINE UP

TEAM		OPPOSING TEAM	
COACH		COACH	

	NO.	STARTERS	POS.		NO.	SUBSTITUTES	POS
1							
2							
3							
4							
5							
6							
7							
8							
9							
10							
11							
12							
13							
14							
15							
16							
17							

NOTES

DATE	TIME	FIELD

BASEBALL / SOFTBALL SCORESHEET

	#	PLAYER	POS	1	2	3	4	5	6	7	8	9
1												
SUB.												
2												
SUB.												
3												
SUB.												
4												
SUB.												
5												
SUB.												
6												
SUB.												
7												
SUB.												
8												
SUB.												
9												
SUB.												
10												
SUB.												
11												
SUB.												
12												
SUB.												
13												
SUB.												
14												
SUB.												
15												
SUB.												
16												
SUB.												
17												
SUB.												TOTALS

INNING TOTALS	RUNS										
	HITS										
	ERRORS										
	LEFT ON BASE										

BASEBALL / SOFTBALL SCORESHEET

AB	R	H	RBI	BB	SO	PLAYER #			
						1 2 3 4 5 6 7 8 9 10 ...	1 2 3 ...	1 2 3 ...	1 2 3 ...

PLAYER #

DATE	START TIME	END TIME
FIELD		

HOME	
VISITOR	

#	PITCHER	W	L	S	IP	BF	H	R	ER	BB	SO
	TOTALS										

PITCHES BY INNING	1	2	3	4	5	6	7	8	9
TOTALS									

NOTES

FINAL SCORE

HOME	VISITOR
RUNS	
HITS	
ERRORS	
UMPIRES	
SCORER	

NOTES

PITCH COUNT TOTALS

TEAM LINE UP

TEAM		OPPOSING TEAM	
COACH		COACH	

	NO.	STARTERS	POS.		NO.	SUBSTITUTES	POS
1							
2							
3							
4							
5							
6							
7							
8							
9							
10							
11							
12							
13							
14							
15							
16							
17							

NOTES		
DATE	TIME	FIELD

BASEBALL / SOFTBALL SCORESHEET

	#	PLAYER	POS	1	2	3	4	5	6	7	8	9
1												
SUB.												
2												
SUB.												
3												
SUB.												
4												
SUB.												
5												
SUB.												
6												
SUB.												
7												
SUB.												
8												
SUB.												
9												
SUB.												
10												
SUB.												
11												
SUB.												
12												
SUB.												
13												
SUB.												
14												
SUB.												
15												
SUB.												
16												
SUB.												
17												
SUB.											TOTALS

INNING TOTALS	RUNS									
	HITS									
	ERRORS									
	LEFT ON BASE									

BASEBALL / SOFTBALL SCORESHEET

AB	R	H	RBI	BB	SO	PLAYER #

PLAYER # columns numbered 1–100 (four columns)

DATE	START TIME	END TIME

FIELD

HOME	
VISITOR	

#	PITCHER	W	L	S	IP	BF	H	R	ER	BB	SO
	TOTALS										

PITCHES BY INNING	1	2	3	4	5	6	7	8	9
TOTALS									

NOTES

FINAL SCORE	
HOME	VISITOR
RUNS	
HITS	
ERRORS	
UMPIRES	
SCORER	

NOTES

PITCH COUNT TOTALS

TEAM LINE UP

TEAM		OPPOSING TEAM	
COACH		COACH	

	NO.	STARTERS	POS.		NO.	SUBSTITUTES	POS
1							
2							
3							
4							
5							
6							
7							
8							
9							
10							
11							
12							
13							
14							
15							
16							
17							

NOTES		
DATE	TIME	FIELD

BASEBALL / SOFTBALL SCORESHEET

	#	PLAYER	POS	1	2	3	4	5	6	7	8	9
1												
SUB.												
2												
SUB.												
3												
SUB.												
4												
SUB.												
5												
SUB.												
6												
SUB.												
7												
SUB.												
8												
SUB.												
9												
SUB.												
10												
SUB.												
11												
SUB.												
12												
SUB.												
13												
SUB.												
14												
SUB.												
15												
SUB.												
16												
SUB.												
17												
SUB.												TOTALS

INNING TOTALS	RUNS									
	HITS									
	ERRORS									
	LEFT ON BASE									

BASEBALL / SOFTBALL SCORESHEET

AB	R	H	RBI	BB	SO	PLAYER #

PLAYER # columns numbered 1–100 (four columns)

DATE	START TIME	END TIME

FIELD

HOME	
VISITOR	

#	PITCHER	W	L	S	IP	BF	H	R	ER	BB	SO
	TOTALS										

PITCHES BY INNING	1	2	3	4	5	6	7	8	9
TOTALS									

NOTES

FINAL SCORE

HOME	VISITOR
RUNS	
HITS	
ERRORS	

UMPIRES	
SCORER	

NOTES

PITCH COUNT TOTALS

TEAM LINE UP

TEAM		OPPOSING TEAM	
COACH		COACH	

	NO.	STARTERS	POS.
1			
2			
3			
4			
5			
6			
7			
8			
9			
10			
11			
12			
13			
14			
15			
16			
17			

NO.	SUBSTITUTES	POS

NOTES		
DATE	TIME	FIELD

BASEBALL / SOFTBALL SCORESHEET

#	PLAYER	POS	1	2	3	4	5	6	7	8	9	
1												
SUB.												
2												
SUB.												
3												
SUB.												
4												
SUB.												
5												
SUB.												
6												
SUB.												
7												
SUB.												
8												
SUB.												
9												
SUB.												
10												
SUB.												
11												
SUB.												
12												
SUB.												
13												
SUB.												
14												
SUB.												
15												
SUB.												
16												
SUB.												
17												TOTALS
SUB.												

INNING TOTALS	RUNS									
	HITS									
	ERRORS									
	LEFT ON BASE									

BASEBALL / SOFTBALL SCORESHEET

AB	R	H	RBI	BB	SO	PLAYER #

PLAYER # columns numbered 1–100 (four columns)

NOTES

PITCH COUNT TOTALS

DATE	START TIME	END TIME

FIELD

HOME	
VISITOR	

#	PITCHER	W	L	S	IP	BF	H	R	ER	BB	SO
	TOTALS										

PITCHES BY INNING	1	2	3	4	5	6	7	8	9
TOTALS									

NOTES

FINAL SCORE		
HOME		VISITOR
	RUNS	
	HITS	
	ERRORS	
UMPIRES		
SCORER		

TEAM LINE UP

TEAM		OPPOSING TEAM	
COACH		COACH	

	NO.	STARTERS	POS.		NO.	SUBSTITUTES	POS
1							
2							
3							
4							
5							
6							
7							
8							
9							
10							
11							
12							
13							
14							
15							
16							
17							

NOTES		
DATE	TIME	FIELD

BASEBALL / SOFTBALL SCORESHEET

	#	PLAYER	POS	1	2	3	4	5	6	7	8	9
1												
SUB.												
2												
SUB.												
3												
SUB.												
4												
SUB.												
5												
SUB.												
6												
SUB.												
7												
SUB.												
8												
SUB.												
9												
SUB.												
10												
SUB.												
11												
SUB.												
12												
SUB.												
13												
SUB.												
14												
SUB.												
15												
SUB.												
16												
SUB.												
17												TOTALS
SUB.												

INNING TOTALS	RUNS										
	HITS										
	ERRORS										
	LEFT ON BASE										

BASEBALL / SOFTBALL SCORESHEET

AB	R	H	RBI	BB	SO	PLAYER #

PLAYER # columns numbered 1 to 100 (four columns)

DATE	START TIME	END TIME

FIELD

HOME	
VISITOR	

#	PITCHER	W	L	S	IP	BF	H	R	ER	BB	SO
	TOTALS										

PITCHES BY INNING	1	2	3	4	5	6	7	8	9
TOTALS									

NOTES

FINAL SCORE	
HOME	VISITOR
RUNS	
HITS	
ERRORS	
UMPIRES	
SCORER	

NOTES

PITCH COUNT TOTALS

TEAM LINE UP

TEAM	OPPOSING TEAM
COACH	COACH

	NO.	STARTERS	POS.		NO.	SUBSTITUTES	POS
1							
2							
3							
4							
5							
6							
7							
8							
9							
10							
11							
12							
13							
14							
15							
16							
17							

NOTES

DATE	TIME	FIELD

BASEBALL / SOFTBALL SCORESHEET

	#	PLAYER	POS	1	2	3	4	5	6	7	8	9
1												
SUB.												
2												
SUB.												
3												
SUB.												
4												
SUB.												
5												
SUB.												
6												
SUB.												
7												
SUB.												
8												
SUB.												
9												
SUB.												
10												
SUB.												
11												
SUB.												
12												
SUB.												
13												
SUB.												
14												
SUB.												
15												
SUB.												
16												
SUB.												
17												TOTALS
SUB.												

INNING TOTALS										
	RUNS									
	HITS									
	ERRORS									
	LEFT ON BASE									

BASEBALL / SOFTBALL SCORESHEET

AB	R	H	RBI	BB	SO		PLAYER #			

PLAYER # columns with numbered rows 1–100 (four columns each numbered 1 to 100)

NOTES

PITCH COUNT TOTALS

DATE	START TIME	END TIME

FIELD

HOME	
VISITOR	

#	PITCHER	W	L	S	IP	BF	H	R	ER	BB	SO
	TOTALS										

PITCHES BY INNING	1	2	3	4	5	6	7	8	9
TOTALS									

NOTES

FINAL SCORE		
HOME		VISITOR
	RUNS	
	HITS	
	ERRORS	
UMPIRES		
SCORER		

TEAM LINE UP

TEAM	OPPOSING TEAM
COACH	COACH

	NO.	STARTERS	POS.		NO.	SUBSTITUTES	POS
1							
2							
3							
4							
5							
6							
7							
8							
9							
10							
11							
12							
13							
14							
15							
16							
17							

NOTES	

DATE	TIME	FIELD

BASEBALL / SOFTBALL SCORESHEET

	#	PLAYER	POS	1	2	3	4	5	6	7	8	9	
1													
SUB.													
2													
SUB.													
3													
SUB.													
4													
SUB.													
5													
SUB.													
6													
SUB.													
7													
SUB.													
8													
SUB.													
9													
SUB.													
10													
SUB.													
11													
SUB.													
12													
SUB.													
13													
SUB.													
14													
SUB.													
15													
SUB.													
16													
SUB.													
17													TOTALS
SUB.													

INNING TOTALS	RUNS									
	HITS									
	ERRORS									
	LEFT ON BASE									

BASEBALL / SOFTBALL SCORESHEET

AB	R	H	RBI	BB	SO	PLAYER #

PLAYER # columns (numbered 1–100, four columns)

DATE	START TIME	END TIME
FIELD		
HOME		
VISITOR		

#	PITCHER	W	L	S	IP	BF	H	R	ER	BB	SO
	TOTALS										

PITCHES BY INNING	1	2	3	4	5	6	7	8	9
TOTALS										

NOTES

FINAL SCORE	
HOME	VISITOR
RUNS	
HITS	
ERRORS	
UMPIRES	
SCORER	

NOTES

PITCH COUNT TOTALS

TEAM LINE UP

TEAM		OPPOSING TEAM	
COACH		COACH	

	NO.	STARTERS	POS.		NO.	SUBSTITUTES	POS
1							
2							
3							
4							
5							
6							
7							
8							
9							
10							
11							
12							
13							
14							
15							
16							
17							

NOTES		
DATE	TIME	FIELD

BASEBALL / SOFTBALL SCORESHEET

	#	PLAYER	POS	1	2	3	4	5	6	7	8	9
1												
SUB.												
2												
SUB.												
3												
SUB.												
4												
SUB.												
5												
SUB.												
6												
SUB.												
7												
SUB.												
8												
SUB.												
9												
SUB.												
10												
SUB.												
11												
SUB.												
12												
SUB.												
13												
SUB.												
14												
SUB.												
15												
SUB.												
16												
SUB.												
17												
SUB.												

INNING TOTALS	RUNS										TOTALS
	HITS										
	ERRORS										
	LEFT ON BASE										

BASEBALL / SOFTBALL SCORESHEET

AB	R	H	RBI	BB	SO		PLAYER #		

PLAYER # columns (1–100 pitch count for each of four players):

1	1	1	1
2	2	2	2
3	3	3	3
4	4	4	4
5	5	5	5
6	6	6	6
7	7	7	7
8	8	8	8
9	9	9	9
10	10	10	10
11	11	11	11
12	12	12	12
13	13	13	13
14	14	14	14
15	15	15	15
16	16	16	16
17	17	17	17
18	18	18	18
19	19	19	19
20	20	20	20
21	21	21	21
22	22	22	22
23	23	23	23
24	24	24	24
25	25	25	25
26	26	26	26
27	27	27	27
28	28	28	28
29	29	29	29
30	30	30	30
31	31	31	31
32	32	32	32
33	33	33	33
34	34	34	34
35	35	35	35
36	36	36	36
37	37	37	37
38	38	38	38
39	39	39	39
40	40	40	40
41	41	41	41
42	42	42	42
43	43	43	43
44	44	44	44
45	45	45	45
46	46	46	46
47	47	47	47
48	48	48	48
49	49	49	49
50	50	50	50
51	51	51	51
52	52	52	52
53	53	53	53
54	54	54	54
55	55	55	55
56	56	56	56
57	57	57	57
58	58	58	58
59	59	59	59
60	60	60	60
61	61	61	61
62	62	62	62
63	63	63	63
64	64	64	64
65	65	65	65
66	66	66	66
67	67	67	67
68	68	68	68
69	69	69	69
70	70	70	70
71	71	71	71
72	72	72	72
73	73	73	73
74	74	74	74
75	75	75	75
76	76	76	76
77	77	77	77
78	78	78	78
79	79	79	79
80	80	80	80
81	81	81	81
82	82	82	82
83	83	83	83
84	84	84	84
85	85	85	85
86	86	86	86
87	87	87	87
88	88	88	88
89	89	89	89
90	90	90	90
91	91	91	91
92	92	92	92
93	93	93	93
94	94	94	94
95	95	95	95
96	96	96	96
97	97	97	97
98	98	98	98
99	99	99	99
100	100	100	100

NOTES

PITCH COUNT TOTALS

DATE	START TIME	END TIME
FIELD		
HOME		
VISITOR		

#	PITCHER	W	L	S	IP	BF	H	R	ER	BB	SO
	TOTALS										

PITCHES BY INNING	1	2	3	4	5	6	7	8	9
TOTALS									

NOTES

FINAL SCORE	
HOME	VISITOR
	RUNS	
	HITS	
	ERRORS	
UMPIRES	
SCORER	

TEAM LINE UP

TEAM	OPPOSING TEAM
COACH	COACH

	NO.	STARTERS	POS.		NO.	SUBSTITUTES	POS
1							
2							
3							
4							
5							
6							
7							
8							
9							
10							
11							
12							
13							
14							
15							
16							
17							

NOTES

DATE	TIME	FIELD

BASEBALL / SOFTBALL SCORESHEET

	#	PLAYER	POS	1	2	3	4	5	6	7	8	9
1												
SUB.												
2												
SUB.												
3												
SUB.												
4												
SUB.												
5												
SUB.												
6												
SUB.												
7												
SUB.												
8												
SUB.												
9												
SUB.												
10												
SUB.												
11												
SUB.												
12												
SUB.												
13												
SUB.												
14												
SUB.												
15												
SUB.												
16												
SUB.												
17												TOTALS
SUB.												

INNING TOTALS	RUNS									
	HITS									
	ERRORS									
	LEFT ON BASE									

Each inning cell contains: 1B 2B 3B HR BB

BASEBALL / SOFTBALL SCORESHEET

AB	R	H	RBI	BB	SO	PLAYER #

PLAYER # columns (four): 1–100 repeated in each of four columns.

DATE	START TIME	END TIME

FIELD

HOME	
VISITOR	

#	PITCHER	W	L	S	IP	BF	H	R	ER	BB	SO
	TOTALS										

PITCHES BY INNING	1	2	3	4	5	6	7	8	9
TOTALS									

NOTES

FINAL SCORE		
HOME		VISITOR
	RUNS	
	HITS	
	ERRORS	
UMPIRES		
SCORER		

TEAM LINE UP

TEAM	OPPOSING TEAM
COACH	COACH

	NO.	STARTERS	POS.		NO.	SUBSTITUTES	POS
1							
2							
3							
4							
5							
6							
7							
8							
9							
10							
11							
12							
13							
14							
15							
16							
17							

NOTES		
DATE	TIME	FIELD

BASEBALL / SOFTBALL SCORESHEET

	#	PLAYER	POS	1	2	3	4	5	6	7	8	9
1												
SUB.												
2												
SUB.												
3												
SUB.												
4												
SUB.												
5												
SUB.												
6												
SUB.												
7												
SUB.												
8												
SUB.												
9												
SUB.												
10												
SUB.												
11												
SUB.												
12												
SUB.												
13												
SUB.												
14												
SUB.												
15												
SUB.												
16												
SUB.												
17												
SUB.											TOTALS

INNING TOTALS	RUNS									
	HITS									
	ERRORS									
	LEFT ON BASE									

BASEBALL / SOFTBALL SCORESHEET

AB	R	H	RBI	BB	SO		PLAYER #			

PLAYER #

						1	1	1	1
						2	2	2	2
						3	3	3	3
						4	4	4	4
						5	5	5	5
						6	6	6	6
						7	7	7	7
						8	8	8	8
						9	9	9	9
						10	10	10	10

(player number columns numbered 1 through 100)

NOTES

PITCH COUNT TOTALS

DATE	START TIME	END TIME

FIELD

HOME	
VISITOR	

#	PITCHER	W	L	S	IP	BF	H	R	ER	BB	SO
	TOTALS										

PITCHES BY INNING	1	2	3	4	5	6	7	8	9
TOTALS									

NOTES

FINAL SCORE

	HOME		VISITOR
	RUNS		
	HITS		
	ERRORS		

UMPIRES	
SCORER	

TEAM LINE UP

TEAM		OPPOSING TEAM	
COACH		COACH	

	NO.	STARTERS	POS.
1			
2			
3			
4			
5			
6			
7			
8			
9			
10			
11			
12			
13			
14			
15			
16			
17			

NO.	SUBSTITUTES	POS

NOTES

DATE	TIME	FIELD

BASEBALL / SOFTBALL SCORESHEET

	#	PLAYER	POS	1	2	3	4	5	6	7	8	9
1												
SUB.												
2												
SUB.												
3												
SUB.												
4												
SUB.												
5												
SUB.												
6												
SUB.												
7												
SUB.												
8												
SUB.												
9												
SUB.												
10												
SUB.												
11												
SUB.												
12												
SUB.												
13												
SUB.												
14												
SUB.												
15												
SUB.												
16												
SUB.												
17												TOTALS
SUB.												

INNING TOTALS	RUNS										
	HITS										
	ERRORS										
	LEFT ON BASE										

BASEBALL / SOFTBALL SCORESHEET

AB	R	H	RBI	BB	SO			PLAYER #		

PLAYER # columns numbered 1 through 100 (four columns)

DATE	START TIME	END TIME
FIELD		

HOME	
VISITOR	

#	PITCHER	W	L	S	IP	BF	H	R	ER	BB	SO
	TOTALS										

PITCHES BY INNING	1	2	3	4	5	6	7	8	9
TOTALS									

NOTES

NOTES

PITCH COUNT TOTALS

FINAL SCORE	
HOME	VISITOR
RUNS	
HITS	
ERRORS	
UMPIRES	
SCORER	

TEAM LINE UP

TEAM		OPPOSING TEAM	
COACH		COACH	

	NO.	STARTERS	POS.
1			
2			
3			
4			
5			
6			
7			
8			
9			
10			
11			
12			
13			
14			
15			
16			
17			

NO.	SUBSTITUTES	POS

NOTES		
DATE	TIME	FIELD

BASEBALL / SOFTBALL SCORESHEET

	#	PLAYER	POS	1	2	3	4	5	6	7	8	9	
1													
SUB.													
2													
SUB.													
3													
SUB.													
4													
SUB.													
5													
SUB.													
6													
SUB.													
7													
SUB.													
8													
SUB.													
9													
SUB.													
10													
SUB.													
11													
SUB.													
12													
SUB.													
13													
SUB.													
14													
SUB.													
15													
SUB.													
16													
SUB.													
17													TOTALS
SUB.													

INNING TOTALS	RUNS										
	HITS										
	ERRORS										
	LEFT ON BASE										

BASEBALL / SOFTBALL SCORESHEET

AB	R	H	RBI	BB	SO			PLAYER #		

PLAYER # columns numbered 1–100 (four columns, each 1 through 100)

NOTES						PITCH COUNT TOTALS

DATE	START TIME	END TIME
FIELD		

HOME	
VISITOR	

#	PITCHER	W	L	S	IP	BF	H	R	ER	BB	SO
	TOTALS										

PITCHES BY INNING	1	2	3	4	5	6	7	8	9
TOTALS									

NOTES

FINAL SCORE	
HOME	VISITOR
RUNS	
HITS	
ERRORS	
UMPIRES	
SCORER	

TEAM LINE UP

TEAM		OPPOSING TEAM	
COACH		COACH	

	NO.	STARTERS	POS.		NO.	SUBSTITUTES	POS
1							
2							
3							
4							
5							
6							
7							
8							
9							
10							
11							
12							
13							
14							
15							
16							
17							

NOTES		
DATE	TIME	FIELD

BASEBALL / SOFTBALL SCORESHEET

	#	PLAYER	POS	1	2	3	4	5	6	7	8	9
1												
SUB.												
2												
SUB.												
3												
SUB.												
4												
SUB.												
5												
SUB.												
6												
SUB.												
7												
SUB.												
8												
SUB.												
9												
SUB.												
10												
SUB.												
11												
SUB.												
12												
SUB.												
13												
SUB.												
14												
SUB.												
15												
SUB.												
16												
SUB.												
17												
SUB.												

INNING TOTALS	RUNS											TOTALS
	HITS											
	ERRORS											
	LEFT ON BASE											

BASEBALL / SOFTBALL SCORESHEET

AB	R	H	RBI	BB	SO		PLAYER #			

PLAYER # columns numbered 1 to 100 (four columns)

DATE	START TIME	END TIME
FIELD		

HOME	
VISITOR	

#	PITCHER	W	L	S	IP	BF	H	R	ER	BB	SO
	TOTALS										

PITCHES BY INNING	1	2	3	4	5	6	7	8	9
TOTALS									

NOTES

FINAL SCORE

	HOME	VISITOR
RUNS		
HITS		
ERRORS		
UMPIRES		
SCORER		

NOTES

PITCH COUNT TOTALS

TEAM LINE UP

TEAM	OPPOSING TEAM
COACH	COACH

	NO.	STARTERS	POS.		NO.	SUBSTITUTES	POS
1							
2							
3							
4							
5							
6							
7							
8							
9							
10							
11							
12							
13							
14							
15							
16							
17							

NOTES		
DATE	TIME	FIELD

BASEBALL / SOFTBALL SCORESHEET

#	PLAYER	POS	1	2	3	4	5	6	7	8	9
1											
SUB.											
2											
SUB.											
3											
SUB.											
4											
SUB.											
5											
SUB.											
6											
SUB.											
7											
SUB.											
8											
SUB.											
9											
SUB.											
10											
SUB.											
11											
SUB.											
12											
SUB.											
13											
SUB.											
14											
SUB.											
15											
SUB.											
16											
SUB.											
17											
SUB.											

TOTALS

INNING TOTALS											
	RUNS										
	HITS										
	ERRORS										
	LEFT ON BASE										

BASEBALL / SOFTBALL SCORESHEET

AB	R	H	RBI	BB	SO		PLAYER #			
							1	1	1	1
							2	2	2	2
							3	3	3	3
							4	4	4	4
							5	5	5	5
							6	6	6	6
							7	7	7	7
							8	8	8	8
							9	9	9	9
							10	10	10	10

(Player # columns continue numbered 1 through 100)

NOTES

PITCH COUNT TOTALS

DATE		START TIME		END TIME	
FIELD					
HOME					
VISITOR					

#	PITCHER	W	L	S	IP	BF	H	R	ER	BB	SO
	TOTALS										

PITCHES BY INNING	1	2	3	4	5	6	7	8	9
TOTALS									

NOTES

FINAL SCORE		
HOME		VISITOR
	RUNS	
	HITS	
	ERRORS	
UMPIRES		
SCORER		

TEAM LINE UP

TEAM		OPPOSING TEAM	
COACH		COACH	

	NO.	STARTERS	POS.
1			
2			
3			
4			
5			
6			
7			
8			
9			
10			
11			
12			
13			
14			
15			
16			
17			

NO.	SUBSTITUTES	POS

NOTES

DATE	TIME	FIELD

BASEBALL / SOFTBALL SCORESHEET

	#	PLAYER	POS	1	2	3	4	5	6	7	8	9
1												
SUB.												
2												
SUB.												
3												
SUB.												
4												
SUB.												
5												
SUB.												
6												
SUB.												
7												
SUB.												
8												
SUB.												
9												
SUB.												
10												
SUB.												
11												
SUB.												
12												
SUB.												
13												
SUB.												
14												
SUB.												
15												
SUB.												
16												
SUB.												
17												
SUB.												TOTALS

INNING TOTALS	RUNS										
	HITS										
	ERRORS										
	LEFT ON BASE										

BASEBALL / SOFTBALL SCORESHEET

AB	R	H	RBI	BB	SO

PLAYER #

1	1	1	1
2	2	2	2
3	3	3	3
4	4	4	4
5	5	5	5
6	6	6	6
7	7	7	7
8	8	8	8
9	9	9	9
10	10	10	10
11	11	11	11
12	12	12	12
13	13	13	13
14	14	14	14
15	15	15	15
16	16	16	16
17	17	17	17
18	18	18	18
19	19	19	19
20	20	20	20
... (21 through 100)

NOTES

PITCH COUNT TOTALS

DATE	START TIME	END TIME

FIELD

| HOME | |
| VISITOR | |

#	PITCHER	W	L	S	IP	BF	H	R	ER	BB	SO
	TOTALS										

PITCHES BY INNING	1	2	3	4	5	6	7	8	9
TOTALS									

NOTES

FINAL SCORE

HOME		VISITOR
	RUNS	
	HITS	
	ERRORS	
UMPIRES		
SCORER		

TEAM LINE UP

TEAM	OPPOSING TEAM
COACH	COACH

	NO.	STARTERS	POS.
1			
2			
3			
4			
5			
6			
7			
8			
9			
10			
11			
12			
13			
14			
15			
16			
17			

NO.	SUBSTITUTES	POS

NOTES		
DATE	TIME	FIELD

BASEBALL / SOFTBALL SCORESHEET

	#	PLAYER	POS	1	2	3	4	5	6	7	8	9	
1													
SUB.													
2													
SUB.													
3													
SUB.													
4													
SUB.													
5													
SUB.													
6													
SUB.													
7													
SUB.													
8													
SUB.													
9													
SUB.													
10													
SUB.													
11													
SUB.													
12													
SUB.													
13													
SUB.													
14													
SUB.													
15													
SUB.													
16													
SUB.													
17													TOTALS
SUB.													

INNING TOTALS											
	RUNS										
	HITS										
	ERRORS										
	LEFT ON BASE										

1B 2B 3B HR BB

BASEBALL / SOFTBALL SCORESHEET

AB	R	H	RBI	BB	SO	PLAYER #

PLAYER # columns numbered 1–100 (four columns)

DATE	START TIME	END TIME

FIELD

HOME	
VISITOR	

#	PITCHER	W	L	S	IP	BF	H	R	ER	BB	SO
	TOTALS										

PITCHES BY INNING	1	2	3	4	5	6	7	8	9
TOTALS										

NOTES

FINAL SCORE

	HOME	VISITOR
	RUNS	
	HITS	
	ERRORS	

UMPIRES	
SCORER	

NOTES

PITCH COUNT TOTALS

TEAM LINE UP

TEAM		OPPOSING TEAM
COACH		COACH

	NO.	STARTERS	POS.		NO.	SUBSTITUTES	POS
1							
2							
3							
4							
5							
6							
7							
8							
9							
10							
11							
12							
13							
14							
15							
16							
17							

NOTES

DATE	TIME	FIELD

BASEBALL / SOFTBALL SCORESHEET

	#	PLAYER	POS	1	2	3	4	5	6	7	8	9
1												
SUB.												
2												
SUB.												
3												
SUB.												
4												
SUB.												
5												
SUB.												
6												
SUB.												
7												
SUB.												
8												
SUB.												
9												
SUB.												
10												
SUB.												
11												
SUB.												
12												
SUB.												
13												
SUB.												
14												
SUB.												
15												
SUB.												
16												
SUB.												
17												
SUB.												TOTALS

INNING TOTALS	RUNS									
	HITS									
	ERRORS									
	LEFT ON BASE									

BASEBALL / SOFTBALL SCORESHEET

AB	R	H	RBI	BB	SO	PLAYER #			

PLAYER # columns numbered 1 through 100 (four columns)

DATE	START TIME	END TIME

FIELD

HOME	
VISITOR	

#	PITCHER	W	L	S	IP	BF	H	R	ER	BB	SO
TOTALS											

PITCHES BY INNING	1	2	3	4	5	6	7	8	9
TOTALS									

NOTES

FINAL SCORE

HOME	VISITOR
RUNS	
HITS	
ERRORS	

UMPIRES	
SCORER	

NOTES

PITCH COUNT TOTALS

TEAM LINE UP

TEAM		OPPOSING TEAM	
COACH		COACH	

	NO.	STARTERS	POS.
1			
2			
3			
4			
5			
6			
7			
8			
9			
10			
11			
12			
13			
14			
15			
16			
17			

NO.	SUBSTITUTES	POS

NOTES		
DATE	TIME	FIELD

BASEBALL / SOFTBALL SCORESHEET

	#	PLAYER	POS	1	2	3	4	5	6	7	8	9
1												
SUB.												
2												
SUB.												
3												
SUB.												
4												
SUB.												
5												
SUB.												
6												
SUB.												
7												
SUB.												
8												
SUB.												
9												
SUB.												
10												
SUB.												
11												
SUB.												
12												
SUB.												
13												
SUB.												
14												
SUB.												
15												
SUB.												
16												
SUB.												
17												
SUB.												

INNING TOTALS	RUNS										TOTALS
	HITS										
	ERRORS										
	LEFT ON BASE										

BASEBALL / SOFTBALL SCORESHEET

AB	R	H	RBI	BB	SO		PLAYER #			

PLAYER #

1	1	1	1
2	2	2	2
3	3	3	3
4	4	4	4
5	5	5	5
6	6	6	6
7	7	7	7
8	8	8	8
9	9	9	9
10	10	10	10
11	11	11	11
12	12	12	12
13	13	13	13
14	14	14	14
15	15	15	15
16	16	16	16
17	17	17	17
18	18	18	18
19	19	19	19
20	20	20	20
21	21	21	21
22	22	22	22
23	23	23	23
24	24	24	24
25	25	25	25
26	26	26	26
27	27	27	27
28	28	28	28
29	29	29	29
30	30	30	30
... (continuing) ... | 100 | 100 | 100 | 100 |

NOTES

PITCH COUNT TOTALS

DATE | START TIME | END TIME

FIELD

HOME

VISITOR

#	PITCHER	W	L	S	IP	BF	H	R	ER	BB	SO
	TOTALS										

PITCHES BY INNING	1	2	3	4	5	6	7	8	9
TOTALS									

NOTES

FINAL SCORE

	HOME		VISITOR
	RUNS		
	HITS		
	ERRORS		
UMPIRES			
SCORER			

TEAM LINE UP

TEAM	OPPOSING TEAM
COACH	COACH

	NO.	STARTERS	POS.		NO.	SUBSTITUTES	POS
1							
2							
3							
4							
5							
6							
7							
8							
9							
10							
11							
12							
13							
14							
15							
16							
17							

NOTES

DATE	TIME	FIELD

BASEBALL / SOFTBALL SCORESHEET

	#	PLAYER	POS	1	2	3	4	5	6	7	8	9	
1													
SUB.													
2													
SUB.													
3													
SUB.													
4													
SUB.													
5													
SUB.													
6													
SUB.													
7													
SUB.													
8													
SUB.													
9													
SUB.													
10													
SUB.													
11													
SUB.													
12													
SUB.													
13													
SUB.													
14													
SUB.													
15													
SUB.													
16													
SUB.													
17													TOTALS
SUB.													

Each batting cell labeled: 1B 2B 3B HR BB

INNING TOTALS	RUNS									
	HITS									
	ERRORS									
	LEFT ON BASE									

BASEBALL / SOFTBALL SCORESHEET

AB	R	H	RBI	BB	SO	PLAYER #

Player # columns numbered 1–100 (four columns).

NOTES

PITCH COUNT TOTALS

DATE	START TIME	END TIME
FIELD		
HOME		
VISITOR		

#	PITCHER	W	L	S	IP	BF	H	R	ER	BB	SO
	TOTALS										

PITCHES BY INNING	1	2	3	4	5	6	7	8	9
TOTALS									

NOTES

FINAL SCORE	
HOME	VISITOR
RUNS	
HITS	
ERRORS	
UMPIRES	
SCORER	

TEAM LINE UP

TEAM		OPPOSING TEAM	
COACH		COACH	

	NO.	STARTERS	POS.		NO.	SUBSTITUTES	POS
1							
2							
3							
4							
5							
6							
7							
8							
9							
10							
11							
12							
13							
14							
15							
16							
17							

NOTES		
DATE	TIME	FIELD

BASEBALL / SOFTBALL SCORESHEET

	#	PLAYER	POS	1	2	3	4	5	6	7	8	9
1												
SUB.												
2												
SUB.												
3												
SUB.												
4												
SUB.												
5												
SUB.												
6												
SUB.												
7												
SUB.												
8												
SUB.												
9												
SUB.												
10												
SUB.												
11												
SUB.												
12												
SUB.												
13												
SUB.												
14												
SUB.												
15												
SUB.												
16												
SUB.												
17												TOTALS
SUB.												

INNING TOTALS	RUNS										
	HITS										
	ERRORS										
	LEFT ON BASE										

BASEBALL / SOFTBALL SCORESHEET

AB	R	H	RBI	BB	SO	PLAYER #			

PLAYER #

(Columns numbered 1–100 in four repeating columns)

NOTES

PITCH COUNT TOTALS

DATE	START TIME	END TIME

FIELD

HOME	
VISITOR	

#	PITCHER	W	L	S	IP	BF	H	R	ER	BB	SO
	TOTALS										

PITCHES BY INNING	1	2	3	4	5	6	7	8	9
TOTALS									

NOTES

FINAL SCORE	
HOME	VISITOR
	RUNS	
	HITS	
	ERRORS	

UMPIRES	
SCORER	

TEAM LINE UP

TEAM		OPPOSING TEAM	
COACH		COACH	

	NO.	STARTERS	POS.		NO.	SUBSTITUTES	POS
1							
2							
3							
4							
5							
6							
7							
8							
9							
10							
11							
12							
13							
14							
15							
16							
17							

NOTES		
DATE	TIME	FIELD

BASEBALL / SOFTBALL SCORESHEET

	#	PLAYER	POS	1	2	3	4	5	6	7	8	9
1												
SUB.												
2												
SUB.												
3												
SUB.												
4												
SUB.												
5												
SUB.												
6												
SUB.												
7												
SUB.												
8												
SUB.												
9												
SUB.												
10												
SUB.												
11												
SUB.												
12												
SUB.												
13												
SUB.												
14												
SUB.												
15												
SUB.												
16												
SUB.												
17												
SUB.												TOTALS

INNING TOTALS	RUNS										
	HITS										
	ERRORS										
	LEFT ON BASE										

BASEBALL / SOFTBALL SCORESHEET

AB	R	H	RBI	BB	SO		PLAYER #			

(Player # columns numbered 1 through 100, four columns)

DATE	START TIME	END TIME

FIELD

HOME	
VISITOR	

#	PITCHER	W	L	S	IP	BF	H	R	ER	BB	SO
	TOTALS										

PITCHES BY INNING	1	2	3	4	5	6	7	8	9
TOTALS									

NOTES

PITCH COUNT TOTALS

NOTES

FINAL SCORE

HOME		VISITOR
	RUNS	
	HITS	
	ERRORS	
UMPIRES		
SCORER		

TEAM LINE UP

TEAM	OPPOSING TEAM
COACH	COACH

	NO.	STARTERS	POS.		NO.	SUBSTITUTES	POS
1							
2							
3							
4							
5							
6							
7							
8							
9							
10							
11							
12							
13							
14							
15							
16							
17							

NOTES

DATE	TIME	FIELD

BASEBALL / SOFTBALL SCORESHEET

	#	PLAYER	POS	1	2	3	4	5	6	7	8	9	
1													
SUB.													
2													
SUB.													
3													
SUB.													
4													
SUB.													
5													
SUB.													
6													
SUB.													
7													
SUB.													
8													
SUB.													
9													
SUB.													
10													
SUB.													
11													
SUB.													
12													
SUB.													
13													
SUB.													
14													
SUB.													
15													
SUB.													
16													
SUB.													
17													TOTALS
SUB.													

INNING TOTALS	RUNS										
	HITS										
	ERRORS										
	LEFT ON BASE										

BASEBALL / SOFTBALL SCORESHEET

AB	R	H	RBI	BB	SO	PLAYER #			
						1	1	1	1
						2	2	2	2
						3	3	3	3
						4	4	4	4
						5	5	5	5
						6	6	6	6
						7	7	7	7
						8	8	8	8
						9	9	9	9
						10	10	10	10
						11	11	11	11
						12	12	12	12
						13	13	13	13
						14	14	14	14
						15	15	15	15
						16	16	16	16
						17	17	17	17
						18	18	18	18
						19	19	19	19
						20	20	20	20
						...	...	...	...
						100	100	100	100

NOTES

PITCH COUNT TOTALS

DATE	START TIME	END TIME
FIELD		

HOME	
VISITOR	

#	PITCHER	W	L	S	IP	BF	H	R	ER	BB	SO
	TOTALS										

PITCHES BY INNING	1	2	3	4	5	6	7	8	9
TOTALS									

NOTES

FINAL SCORE		
HOME		VISITOR
	RUNS	
	HITS	
	ERRORS	
UMPIRES		
SCORER		

Made in the USA
Monee, IL
02 August 2022